# The Dude's Meal Prep Manual

By
**David Snedden**

With
**Brian Baker**

*I would like to thank my wife, Dani, for her support and letting me test recipes on her. Thank you to my brother, Josh, for always being my sounding board, and my Uncle Paul for generating my interest in cooking. I would also like to thank my friend and teammate, Brian, who put up with my antics and is the reason this book exists. Without him this is book would still be just an idea.*

**— Dave**


*I would like to thank my family and all my friends, mentors, coaches, and supporters who have helped me along my journey.*

**— Brian**

*"The strength of the pack is the wolf, and the strength of the wolf is the pack."*

**— Rudyard Kipling**

# Table of Contents

# Foreword

At 64 years of age, I am a "dude," and divorced. I found myself "clueless" in the kitchen; after relying on my ex-wife to shoulder my family's nourishment needs for twenty-five years. Cooking was not my thing although healthy eating was, or so I thought. Seven years as a divorced "dude" eating out, taking out, chasing food every day and relying on others to plan, purchase, prepare, and present my meals to me is not really healthy and certainly not true "nourishment." You see, although I appreciated the love that all the chefs and food preparers put into their meals for me, the fact was, the meals were their meals, not mine, and I was disconnected from food and the beneficial aspects of gathering, preparing, serving and purposefully eating it. As Marc David so eloquently wrote in his book **Nourishing Wisdom**, "Ultimately, the most important aspect of nutrition is not what to eat but how our relationship to food can teach us who we are and how we can sustain ourselves at the deepest level of being." Honestly, I was not able to sustain myself at any level of being and did not know how to select, prepare, cook and serve meals for myself, let alone others. I needed help and a solution to my problem. I found it.

I have known Brian Baker for seven years through my association with the Todd Durkin Mastermind Life and Business Coaching program. Brian is an intelligent, passionate, ambitious and successful strength and conditioning coach and trainer and business entrepreneur. I respect Brian's drive, pursuit of excellence and optimal performance in his professional and personal life. When Brian told me that he and his best friend, David Snedden, were writing a book to help "dudes" to prepare and cook food, I was immediately captivated and begged Brian to tell me more. You see, I knew my prayers were answered and I told Brian I would pay any price for their "dude-saver" manual or whatever the name of the book was going to be! I was hungry, in more ways than one and anxious to read and digest everything in their book.

I am happy to report that thanks to David and Brian's ***The Dude's Meal Prep Manual*** I can now cook, and actually have a kitchen stocked with utensils, pots, pans, herbs, spices, and FOOD in the refrigerator and in the pantry, not just cans of V-8. This "dude" now knows how to brown, sauté, caramelize and sear. I know what a slotted spoon, whisk, v-slicer and probe thermometer are. I know how to buy, plan and cook breakfast, lunch and dinner and can prepare healthy snacks. I can store my food for travel and have saved time, energy and money eating my own meals. ***The Dude's Meal Prep Manual*** has improved my health, my social and dating life (women dig dudes who can cook), my sleep and my ability to sustain myself at a deeper level of being. Food is medicine especially when you have a healthy relationship with it.

Thank you, David and Brian, two AWEsome younger "dudes" who empowered this older dude to learn more about food and himself in the process. AND to all you "dudes" out there (and women who have "dudes" in your lives), turn the page and start reading.

See you all in the kitchen!

**Lawrence Indiviglia, MBA, MA**
*Platinum Level Coach for Todd Durkin Enterprises*
*President, INDsightsForLife Inc*

# Introduction

## Why this book?

This book was developed out of passion and necessity. David and Brian are best friends and were roommates in college. They have always shared a love of sports and exercise. Dave has always had a passion for cooking, even as far back as those college days. Dave was always watching cooking shows on the Food Network like Alton Brown and Iron Chef. He developed his love of cooking from his Uncle Paul, who always cooked during family gatherings. Then he discovered the show "Good Eats," and fell in love with the science of cooking. There he learned the global concepts of cooking and how to apply them to his own creations. Meanwhile, Brian could be found watching ESPN or Bear Grylls and eating a frozen pizza.

Fast forward over a decade. Brian and Dave have found their own separate paths, but still remain close friends. Dave became a strength and conditioning coach and has worked at the collegiate level and in Minor League baseball. Brian became a personal trainer and has worked with leaders in business, politics, and entertainment.

Dave is always talking about cooking. He might even love it more than powerlifting. He's always thinking up a new recipe and using it to wow his wife, Dani. Brian, on the other hand, fell into the trap of being an overworked guy who often didn't take the time to cook. When he did, the results were lackluster, to say the least. He knew that cooking was healthier and less expensive, but he didn't know where to start.

Most "healthy" recipes are too fancy and require expensive ingredients, Brian thought. He would go to the grocery store with an extensive shopping list, wandering all over, looking for stuff he had never bought before. He would spend a fortune and almost never used the fancy stuff again. There had to be a better way—a system that would save time, energy, and money. But the food had to be healthy, inexpensive, taste good, be easy to prepare, and support the lives of busy people who work hard and play hard.

After visiting Dave one day, Brian told him, "You should really write a cookbook. I would buy it." But like Brian's cooking, Dave didn't know where to start. Take two dudes who are both into health and performance, one a cook, one a writer, and BAM! The Meal Prep Manual was born.

The next logical step is to spread this knowledge in order to do the most good. Time is a non-renewable resource, energy is always conserved, and money is printed every day. Your health is priceless. We didn't want to just sell you junk. We want to enable you to enjoy health and wealth while living your best life possible.

## Why this system?

Because recipes aren't enough, just like you need a strength and conditioning program versus a workout. A program lasts for weeks or months and is a coherent strategy. A workout is a one-time deal. You can use it multiple times, but results diminish over time.

Combine multiple workouts in a balanced and systematic way, and BAM! You've got a program. That's what we've created here.

## Where are the pictures?

Sticking to the theme of the Manual, we opted to forgo the time and expense of including pretty pictures of food. You can always get those on Instagram. We decided that we could offer you better value by keeping the print version black and white and that ultimately you wanted a system to save you time, energy, and money, not pictures of food.

There you have it. Everything you need. Nothing you don't.

## How to Use the Manual

There are two parts to the manual. Part I shows you how to get properly set up. You'll learn about essential tools, when, where, and what to buy, food storage techniques, and finally some examples of how you can put these together to build your own custom meal plan that is easy, affordable, and convenient.

Part II has a selection of favorite recipes selected by Dave and Brian (mostly Dave). These are the recipes that we like and use. They provide us with good energy, flavor, and variety. Don't like the recipes? Have a food allergy? No problem! You can always substitute your own. We are simply providing you with the system. You can use it to build whatever you want.

Let's get to it.

# Part I

# Gathering Supplies

Chapter 1

# Preparing
# Your Workspace

# Getting to Know Your Equipment for the Kitchen

## Essential Pots and Pans

**Skillet**—This is a pan with gently sloping sides. We suggest one in the 9"-10" range, of the non-stick variety, if you're only going to have one. We recommend a 12" skillet and an 8" with a ceramic coating, making it fantastic for cooking eggs.

**Sauté**—This pan has 2"-3" tall sides that are vertical. We suggest having one that is non-stick, 12" with a matching lid.

**1 Quart Pot**—This is about 6" in diameter and has tall sides; a matching lid is a must as it is used primarily for cooking liquids.

**5 Quart Pot**—This is a large pot and should have a matching lid. You will use this primarily for cooking soups and pastas.

If you buy a set, you can get multiple pieces for a fair price. These sets will often come with more than what I have listed above.

**Baking Sheets**—Available in various sizes. We recommend three sizes: 8", 12", and 18".

**Baking Pan**—Made in a variety of materials: metal, ceramic and glass. We recommend a glass one with a lid, so you can store the food you cook in it.

**Muffin Pan**—These come in a variety of materials now. Some are metal and others are silicone. Silicone is non-stick and flexible but may be slightly more expensive.

**Pizza Round**—Round baking sheet, good for baking foods on, and essential for cutting that occasional frozen pizza.

**Cooling Rack**—This is an optional item that can be used for cooling items out of the oven such as baked goods or even meat.

## Optional Pots and Pans

**Cast Iron Skillet**—We highly recommend a 12" cast iron skillet because of its versatility. Since it is made of iron, you can put it in the oven and on the grill, or even in a fire if you want. Iron pans are sturdy, but are not non-stick, and are tedious to care for. They take a while to get hot, but they retain heat and disperse it evenly.

### Care for your cast iron

1. Prep for initial use: Wash with soap and water. New cast iron is covered in a wax to protect the iron from rust and needs to be removed.

2. Seasoning: Rub your skillet with a thin coat of oil (we prefer to use lard). Place in a cold oven face down with a pan on a rack beneath it to catch any drippings. Heat oven to 350 degrees. Once the oven reaches that temperature, set your timer for 60 minutes. Once time is up, turn off the heat and let the pan cool. Once cool, wipe excess oil with a paper towel.

3. Do not wash with soap and water. With normal use, just rinse with warm water and use a brush or scraper. After the initial seasoning, there is no need to wash with soap and water unless

you have not maintained your pan, and it is starting to rust. If it is rusting, wash and re-season.

4. To clean really stuck-on food, return it to low heat and add coarse kosher salt and about one tablespoon of vegetable oil. Use a pair of tongs and a balled-up paper towel. Use the paper towel to scrub the pan with the salt. Once you have removed any stuck-on food, dump the salt into your sink. Rinse, then dry the pan with a clean towel and return the pan to the heat source, adding one tablespoon of vegetable oil. With a new piece of paper towel, spread the oil all over the inside, outside, bottom, and handle of the pan. Remove from heat. You will know your pan is well seasoned when it is dark black and shiny.

**Tea Kettle**—A tea kettle is good to have for boiling water for various uses: tea, cleaning drains, et cetera.

## Essential Utensils

**Can Opener**—This one is pretty easy to understand. Some of the best can openers are the cheap $2 ones.

**Spatula**—We like one with a silicone head. We find them flexible, making it easier to get under foods, and silicon is relatively heat proof.

**Wooden Spoons**—We like wooden spoons because they're terrible conductors of heat and you don't have to worry about it melting. You can burn one, but you pretty much have to put it in a fire.

**Slotted Spoon**—A slotted spoon is great for serving foods when you don't want excess liquid in the food. They have 2-3 openings in the spoon which allow liquids to pass through.

**Ladle**—A ladle is a large, bowl-like spoon that is great for serving soups and sauces. Typically, the handle is long for reaching into tall pots.

**Measuring Cups and Spoons**—These are needed to measure ingredients. The essential cup sizes you need are ¼, ⅓ and 1 cup. Often a set will have a ½ cup and ¾ cup as well. Measuring spoons are smaller and are found in teaspoon (tsp.) and tablespoon (tbsp.) sizes. They are found in the same range amounts as cups. You can buy measuring cups and spoons separately from each other or together in a set. We prefer metal because they don't stain like plastic will.

**Tongs**—Great for flipping a large piece of meat and tossing pasta and vegetables in sauces. Metal is best due to its heat resistance.

**Colander**—This is a plastic or metal bowl with holes in it to let liquids through. Primarily used for draining pasta, it is also great for washing fruits and vegetables.

**Mixing bowls**—Large bowls of various sizes available in plastic, glass or metal. You can use a set of plastic bowls that double as mixing bowls—but keep a metal one on hand for home-popped popcorn.

**Shaker bottle**—you might have one of these already or see people carrying them around the gym. These are typically plastic and hold about 20 ounces. Not only do they come in handy at the gym, but you can use them in your workshop—I mean kitchen, too.

**Mason Jars**—These come in a variety of sizes and have a variety of uses. Mostly they are used for storage and preserving foods. We recommend having at least five on hand, with lids, in the 32-ounce size.

## Optional Utensils

**Noodle Spoon**—This spoon (also known as a pasta scoop) is large and bowl-like and has spikes coming off the sides. It is great for scooping pasta, but not a necessity.

**Cheese Grater**—We recommend a box grater. This has four sides and each side will allow you to grate in different shapes and sizes. Often it also slices and has three different shredding sizes. Used primarily for cheese, you can also grate root vegetables with it.

**Egg Slicer**—This is a hinged device with taut wires spanning across a gap. This is a great tool for slicing hard-boiled eggs, mushrooms and various fruits. You can do this with a knife, but this tool makes it more convenient.

**Whisk**—We recommend a wire whisk made out of metal. This is great for mixing liquids that need thorough integration, but sometimes a fork works just as well.

**Salad Spinner**—This is great for cleaning and storing lettuce and leafy greens.

**Meat Mallet**—Heavy, made of metal and has smooth and spiked sides. Great for making a piece of meat thinner for stuffing and rolling.

**Digital Scale**—Used for measuring ingredients or divvying up your food into appropriate serving sizes.

**Latex Gloves**—These are great for handling raw meat and spicy peppers. Other choices are nitrile or vinyl for those who have a latex allergy.

# Essential Knives

**Chef's Knife**—Get one in the 6"-8" range to start. A chef's knife has a long tall blade that curves up to a tip at the end. It is a great all-around knife for chopping and cutting meats and vegetables. We would say to start with one knife, and as you become more skilled, add some knives for specific purposes, such as a carving knife.

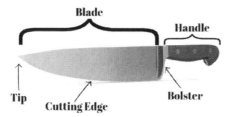

**Cutting Boards**—The rule of thumb for cutting boards is the size of the board should be appropriate for the size of the knife. When you lay your knife down on the board with the handle pointing in one corner and the tip on an angle across the board, there should be a minimum of 2" on either side of the knife to the edge of the board. If there is more, that's okay, if there is less, get a bigger board or smaller knife.

As for materials, there are two appropriate materials for a cutting board; wood and polycarbonate. Wood comes in many forms, from hard maple to bamboo, and now even recycled wood composites. The other choice is polycarbonate; polycarbonate is essentially a form of durable plastic. We recommend having several cutting boards for various purposes; you can buy the four-pack of flexible cutting mats which are inexpensive and easy to replace. We choose these because they come in multiple colors; red for raw meats, green for fruits and vegetables, yellow for cooked meats, and blue for anything else.

Cutting boards come in more materials than just wood and polycarbonate. These materials include glass, metal, and granite. These materials are bad for your knives because they can dull and damage blades, and as we'll discuss later, a dull knife is a dangerous knife.

**Pizza Cutter**—Pretty self-explanatory, you'll need one to slice up the occasional frozen pizza. It's also a useful tool for cutting other things, like dough and leafy herbs.

## Optional Knives

**Kitchen Shears**—These are scissors, yet they are not the scissors you'll find in your mother's sewing kit. They are made of good quality steel and often have a mildly serrated blade for grabbing onto foods. When purchasing a pair, you want a set that breaks into two pieces, one for each handle and blade. You want one that comes apart so that when cutting raw meat you can thoroughly clean the area where the blades overlap, preventing the growth of food-borne bacteria. These are optional but are a great tool for breaking down whole chickens. They can also be used to cut up leafy vegetables and opening food packages.

**Santoku Knife**—Similar in use and shape to a chef's knife, this blade is a Japanese shaped chef's knife. It differs from a chef's knife in that it is flatter and has less of a curve to the tip than a chef's knife. We prefer this knife to a chef's knife when cutting raw meats.

**V-Slicer** – Also known as a mandolin, a v-slicer is great for getting evenly-sliced vegetables. They will often come with multiple inserts to adjust for food thickness and even julienned slices. Use the hand guard they come with—it's there for a reason and can help keep those digits safe!

## Essential Cooking Devices

**Slow Cooker**—Often referred to by its trademarked name, Crock-pot. These are great for soups, stews, and slow cooking meats. We would recommend one in the six-quart size as it's big enough for a large piece of meat. Slow cookers with manual controls are typically less expensive than those with digital controls. It should have at least a high and low setting; a "Keep Warm" one is great but not necessary.

**Blender**—A blender is great for making smoothies and other drinks. It can also be used to blend soups to adjust texture but check with your user manual to see if it can hold hot liquids. Don't necessarily have to break the bank here, but the models that cost more usually have sharper blades and a more powerful motor.

## Optional Cooking Devices

**Instant Pot®**—An Instant Pot® is an electric pressure cooker that has a variety of uses. A pressure cooker will allow you to cook various meats and stocks in a shorter period of time than other methods. From the Instant Pot® website, "Food and liquid are sealed into an airtight vessel, and no steam is released before the pre-set pressure is reached. The boiling point of water increases as the pressure increases, so pressure built up inside the cooker allows the liquid inside to boil at a temperature higher than 100°C / 212°F." In addition to being a pressure cooker, an Instant Pot® can also be used as a rice cooker, slow cooker, and yogurt maker.

**Coffee Grinder**—Its primary use is grinding coffee but is also great for grinding your own herbs and spices.

**Electric Kettle**—An easy way to boil water; just fill it and push the ON button. The machine will shut off when the water is boiling. Fancier models have temperature settings.

**Probe Thermometer**—A probe thermometer is a great tool for cooking roasts by determining the inner temperature, as opposed to cooking for a certain amount of time based on the weight of the roast. You set the desired temperature of the thermometer and insert it into the meat. When the roast reaches the desired temperature, the thermometer will alert you.

**Hand Mixer**—A useful tool used primarily for baking. This makes mixing easier; if you have ever tried to mix your own cake by hand it can get quite tiring.

# Chapter 2

# Building Materials

# When, Where, and What to Buy

## Cooking Equipment

### When

When should you buy your cooking equipment? It's important to start with the essentials. Some pots and pans, and utensils to move food around. You should start with a basic set of pots and pans which can be easily procured from a big box store, as well as boxed sets of utensils. A boxed set of utensils typically contains some spoons, tongs, and spatulas and often comes with a storage unit. As for knives and cutting boards, start with one good chef's knife in the 6"-8" range, and we like the flexible cutting boards due to their price point. As you get into cooking more, you can start to add higher-priced items like a cast iron pan, slow cooker or even and Instant Pot®.

### Where

Where should you purchase your cooking equipment? The obvious answer is any big box store, but we recommend going to a specialty store. Specialty stores would be Bed Bath and Beyond or a restaurant supply store. These two stores are great options because they will carry the widest variety of cooking gear at various price points. In addition, to that they will be staffed by people who have in-depth knowledge of the product and can answer your questions.

### What

What should you start with as a beginner? As we mentioned earlier, start with a basic set of pots and pans. As you advance your cooking skills, you can purchase better pots and pans. More expensive cookware is constructed out of higher-quality materials and disperses heat more evenly. As for utensils, start with the basics, and add more as you need them. Also, go with materials which are heat resistant and won't melt when you go to flip food. When it comes to knives, start with one chef's knife. As your skills improve and you need knives for specific tasks, then look into getting a high-quality set. Keep your knives sharp! Consider an inexpensive knife sharpener or honing tool. As for cutting boards, we prefer the flexible ones, but over time have added a wooden butcher's block for cutting produce. As for specialty equipment such as slow cookers and blenders, buy nice and never buy twice.

## Food

### When

When you should buy depends on what you are cooking that week and what you need. To start with, make sure you have the essential herbs and spices in your cabinet. As for meats, we recommend buying larger packages since they typically cost less per pound than smaller packages. Just don't buy so much that you don't have enough room to store it all in a freezer. As for fruits and vegetables, buy fresh for the things you'll be using that week, but primarily purchase frozen vegetables for convenience.

## Where

Where you purchase your foods from is up to you. You could purchase your food from ALDI, and no, they are not paying us to say this. Dave prefers ALDI for several reasons, primarily that they typically have the best prices. The downside to ALDI is they do not carry specialty items due to their business model (at the time of this publication). If ALDI does not have an item you are looking for, you could go to your regional grocer. In addition, a great place to find good quality cuts of meat and a wide selection is an actual butcher's shop. Being a specialty store, they will have a wide variety of cuts and a staff educated in the product. During the warmer summer months, seek out local farmers markets for your produce. By doing this, you can support small businesses and get high-quality products.

## What

What you should buy is dependent on several factors. To start with, let's discuss what you should be buying. When it comes to produce, try to buy local. Additionally, buy organic produce if it's in your budget. Why organic? Because pesticides, herbicides, estrogen and other chemicals can have nasty effects on the human body. If you don't believe me, read **Estrogeneration** by Dr. Anthony Jay. As for meats, local grown is always best, especially if you can find a farmer who raises their livestock the way nature intended them to be raised. Cattle should be raised strictly on grass; when cattle are fed grass from the time they are weaned until slaughter, they are shown to have a more favorable fat profile. Also, cattle grown that way are typically not fed antibiotics and various hormones. When it comes to pork, responsibly raised pork should be raised similarly to cattle in that they should not be fed in feedlots to promote growth but allowed to graze on acorns and other various food that pigs would eat in the wild. Chickens ideally will be allowed to eat out in fields where they have access to bugs and other such food. Fish is different; wild-caught fish are great if you have access to them, although more and more you are seeing sustainably farmed fish in supermarkets. Great options for fish which can be sustainably farmed are catfish and trout. Large predatory fish such as tuna and salmon are harder to raise in such a way, and often carry higher levels of heavy metals and toxins. Seek out fish that is raised in the good old USA and not China. Why? Primarily, because China has been known to have lax safety practices when it comes to raising fish and livestock.

## Cooking and Shopping

### *When*

When you purchase and cook your food is up to you. Being successful in implementing this system is all about routine. Pick a day to go grocery shopping and try to stick to that every week. We recommend going shopping every Friday. As for prepping your meals, pick one or two days to do it. You can prep your lunches for the week every Sunday. As for dinner, ideally you would cook your dinners every night. If that does not work for you, pick one day to cook two-three dinners for the week, and a second night to cook the rest of your dinners.

### Where

This one is fairly obvious. Purchase your foods from wherever you like. As for cooking them, stick to your kitchen, Unless, of course, you're a guest and get to make a mess in someone else's kitchen.

### What

What you cook is up to you. We have laid out some guidelines to follow in this book with recipes and a suggested meal plan. But at the end of the day, find what you like to eat and plan your own meal plan with those items.

# Chapter 3

# The Nuts and Bolts

# What Holds Everything Together
## (Spicing Up Your Meals)

The items listed here are things you need to bring your food flavor. Some of them listed will have a brief explanation, but for the most part, they won't. Also, the herbs and spices will be divided up into what size you should buy based on usage.

**Coarse Kosher Salt**—This type of salt consists of larger grains than table salt. You will use it primarily for seasoning food before cooking. It's typically available in 48-ounce. and 24-ounce packages; I would go ahead and buy the 48-ounce package, since salt lasts just about forever as long as it doesn't get wet.

**Table Salt**—This is the salt you will use when salting food at the table. It's a relatively fine grain and contains iodine. Iodine is an essential nutrient for preventing goiters, and aids in the production of thyroid hormone. Without getting too scientific, thyroid hormone is what sets the body's metabolism.

# Spices

Spices are parts of plants that contain volatile oils and are used to flavor foods. The only part of the plant eliminated from being a spice are the leaves which are considered herbs. Herbs will be discussed later. The best way to purchase spices are whole and to grind them yourself, since the oils are volatile and begin to degrade as soon as the plant is ground. Since spice shops are not commonly found and whole spices can be pricey, I recommend buying them pre-ground for those who are on a budget.

**Spice list**—The spice list is divided into two sections based on what size to buy. The size to buy is based on usage.

.75-ounce container

Pepper grinder

Chili powder

Onion powder

Paprika

Cumin

Garlic powder

Red pepper flakes

**Garlic Powder**—Get garlic powder, not garlic salt. If you get garlic salt, the salt in the spice will throw off the flavor of the recipe.

**Pepper Grinder**—Most stores sell whole peppercorns in a grinder. The typical size is about 1.75 ounce as opposed to the .75-ounce container for the rest of the spices listed here.

.25-ounce container

Ginger

Cayenne

## Herbs

Herbs are leaves of plants used for their oils to provide flavor to foods.

<u>*75-ounce container*</u>

Italian seasoning

Oregano

<u>*25-ounce container*</u>

Parsley flakes

Thyme

Dill

Rosemary

# Other

These are other powder-like substances to keep on hand for recipes.

**Corn Starch**—Used primarily as a thickening agent in soups and sauces.

**Baking Soda**—Used as a leavening agent in baking. I also keep two open boxes on hand, one in the fridge and one in my cabinets. It acts to help keep funky odors to a minimum and can be helpful in cleaning.

**Baking Powder**—Also used as a leavening agent in baking, it contains baking soda and cream of tartar.

**Flour**—Used primarily in baking, but also can be used to thicken gravies or make a roux.

**Brown Sugar**—Comes in light and dark versions. Brown sugar is white sugar with light or dark molasses added. If you're watching your sugar intake, Splenda and Stevia variations are available.

**Sugar**—Used primarily in baking and to sweeten some recipes.

**Garlic**—You can buy whole heads of garlic if you choose. I have been buying the minced garlic in a glass jar. The flavor isn't as pungent as fresh, but the convenience factor is huge.

### Prepping your own garlic

1. Peel the number of cloves you need from a head of garlic.
2. Lay them on a cutting board.
3. Place the side of your chef's knife on the cloves.
4. Give the knife a good smack with the base of your palm.
5. Peel papery skin away from garlic cloves.
6. Lay on board and mince.

# Liquids

I use "liquids" here for lack of a better term. These are primarily oils and vinegars used in recipes.

**Extra Virgin Olive Oil**—Extra Virgin Olive Oil (EVOO) is from the first press of the olives. Since it is not a refined oil, it has a low smoke point and isn't the best for cooking. I would buy it in a dark glass container, or, if you want to spend the money, buy it in a metal container. UV rays negatively impact oils.

**Apple Cider Vinegar**—Apple Cider Vinegar, ACV for short, is used in the salad dressing recipe. Buy the ACV with a "mother" in it, the floaty-cloudy stuff found at the bottom. The mother is the microbes used to ferment apple cider into vinegar and provides some health benefits to your gut.

**Coconut Oil**—This oil is saturated, meaning it is solid at room temperature. I use this as my primary cooking oil due to its high smoke point and neutral flavor. Also, coconut oil is primarily made up of medium chain triglycerides.

**Soy Sauce or Bragg's Aminos**—Used a lot in our Asian dishes. I like Bragg's Aminos better due to the fact that it is a higher-quality product than mass-produced soy sauces. In addition, I find the Bragg's tastes saltier than traditional soy sauces; just something to keep in mind when adding to food.

**Sesame Oil**—A distinctly flavored oil used in Asian dishes. This oil has a high smoke point and is good for stir fry

**Rice Wine Vinegar**—An Asian vinegar. I use this in my Asian-flavored salad dressing

**Red Wine Vinegar**—Vinegar made from, well, red wine. Great in Greek or Italian style dressings.

**Worcestershire**—A salty, slightly spicy liquid. This goes great as a dipping sauce for red meats and can be used in marinades.

## Condiments

**Ketchup**—Don't think this needs much of an explanation.

**Mustard**—Mustard comes in a lot of varieties. I keep a brown and yellow mustard on hand. I use the brown in my salad dressings as an emulsifier; this helps keep the oil and vinegar from separating. The yellow mustard, I use on burgers.

**BBQ Sauce**—Pick one you like and use it as a dipping sauce or glaze on meats.

**Hot Sauce**—Hot sauce comes in a ton of varieties, I usually keep several styles on hand, usually an American tabasco or Louisiana hot sauce, Mexican such as a Cholula, and Asian, Sriracha.

# Chapter 4

# Using Your Tools

# Safety

**Caution:** When using a knife, safety is your #1 priority. Always use care and precision when handling anything sharp or potentially dangerous. By using this manual, you accept responsibility for your own safety.

1. **Always** use a sharp knife. Dull knives are more likely to slip off food creating a dangerous situation.

2. **Always** use an appropriately sized cutting board for the knife you're using. This was addressed in an earlier chapter.

3. **Always** make sure your cutting board is level and is not going to slide around on the countertop or work surface.

## Knife Grips

There are two primary knife grips. You will use the sword grip and the pinch grip. For the sword grip, grab the handle of the knife in all four fingers and wrap your thumb around. This is primarily used when hacking apart cuts of meat or large vegetables. The second grip is a pinch grip. In the pinch grip, you will pinch the blade of the knife between your thumb and index finger just in front of the bolster and grab the handle with your remaining three fingers. This grip allows for better control over the blade.

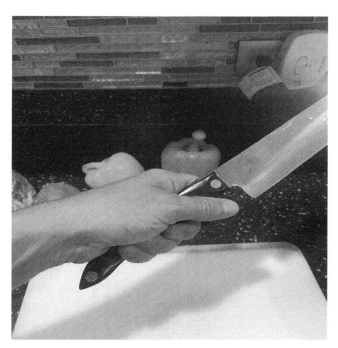

Sword Grip

Pinch Grip (Back)

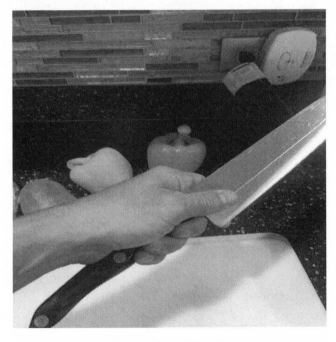

Pinch Grip (Front)

# Cutting Techniques

## *Slice*

Slicing is the cutting of meat or vegetables in such a way that you're cutting the whole piece into thin slices.

## *Chop*

Chopping is cutting your food, typically vegetables, into roughly similarly-sized-pieces that are bite-sized.

## Dice

Dicing is what it sounds like, cutting your meat or vegetables into even cubes. When I dice a larger vegetable, like a potato, I start by cutting it into a more manageable size before I start.

## *Mince*

Mincing is similar to dicing in that you're trying to get the object into small, cube-like pieces. The primary difference is that a mince is smaller and does not need to be as precise. This cut will primarily be used on garlic and occasionally onions.

**Caring for your tools:** Don't put your knives in a dishwasher

1. They're sharp.
2. You don't want them to rattle around and get dull.

## Cooking Methods

### *Brown*

Typically done with meats. This is basically breaking up the meat into pieces and browning the meat on the outside.

### *Sauté*

Cooking in some fat, on relatively high heat.

### *Sweat*

Typically done with onions. This is cooking the onion in fat until it is slightly translucent and glistening with the liquid that is held in the onion.

### *Carmelize*

Typically done with onions. This is cooking the onion slowly in fat until the onions are brown on the outside. The onion browns from the natural sugars found in the onion.

### *Sear*

This is a method done with meat. The outside of the meat will brown and develop a little bit of a crust. The key is to put the meat over relatively high heat and not touch it for 30-60 seconds. This is also the key to developing grill marks on food.

### *Pasta*

Try this cold-water method of cooking pasta! Place one serving of pasta (2 oz. by weight) in one pint of water and salt in an appropriately sized cooking vessel. If I am cooking one to two servings, I do it in a 12" sauté pan. Four servings will need a 5-quart pot. Cover the pot or pan with a well-fitting lid and cook over medium-high heat. Once the water reaches a boil, reduce heat to low and cook for 4-5 minutes, or until al dente ("to the tooth" with a slight firmness in the center). More pasta will need more time. I add a little bit of olive oil to my water to reduce the likelihood of boil overs and to keep the pasta from sticking.

### Simmer

Heat on low to medium-low heat, depending on burner size and amount of water or sauce being used. Try to maintain the temperature of the liquid where it is just barely bubbling.

### Boil

Heat over high heat until bubbling vigorously.

# Chapter 5

# When the Job is Done

## Storage Techniques

### Containers

If you're going to prep food for a few days, it is important to have proper storage containers.

**Containers**—You have basically two options, glass and plastic. Plastic is more affordable than glass but does not last as long. The amount to buy initially is up to how much food you're going to prep ahead of time. I would also invest in one or two glass containers for reheating food, as plastic can leach nasty chemicals into your food. Also, depending on the style you buy, the glass may come with microwave-safe lids.

**Plastic Bags**—If you're going to invest in buying fresh meats in bulk, I would invest in freezer bags. This allows you to divvy up the meat into meal-sized bags for freezer storage.

*Food*

| Refrigerator | | | |
|---|---|---|---|
| *Mushrooms | Berries | Sliced melons | Plums |
| Broccoli | Artichokes | Radishes | Green beans |
| Carrots | Leafy greens | Lettuce | Apricots |
| Cauliflower | Beets | Peas | Cantaloupe |
| Corn | Brussels sprouts | Green onions | Celery |

*Mushrooms should be kept in a paper bag in the fridge.

| Cool Dry Place | | |
|---|---|---|
| Potatoes | Onions | Squash |

Potatoes and onions need to be kept separate. When kept near each other, onions cause potatoes to rot.

| Countertop | | | | |
|---|---|---|---|---|
| Cucumbers | Eggplants | Citrus | Watermelon | Apples |
| Bananas | Tomatoes | Peppers | Garlic | Avocado |

**Ethylene Gas**—Some fruits produce ethylene gas, which can increase how fast some fruits and vegetables ripen and spoil. These need to be kept separate from others. The fruits and vegetables highlighted in green are ethylene producers.

## Meat Storage

Meat should always be stored in the refrigerator or freezer. If you are keeping meat in the refrigerator, place it in a bowl as close to the bottom as possible. This reduces the likelihood of the meat dripping juices over fresh produce, potentially contaminating it.

If you're going to purchase fresh meats in bulk, then you're going to need a storage strategy. You can purchase Ziploc freezer bags with the plastic zipper in both quart and gallon sizes. Then divvy up your meats into the portion sizes you prefer to cook them. Place them into the appropriate-size bag and remove as much air as you can before sealing. Once sealed, you can place them in the freezer until use. You should be able to keep a frozen piece of meat for six to nine months assuming proper storage, but you shouldn't need to keep anything that long because you're cooking on a regular basis.

## Prepped Food Storage

So, you've cooked and prepped all this food, now what to do with it? While we've already discussed having plenty of containers to store your food in, you have two options, depending on the amount of containers that you have.

Option 1: Keep prepped food together according to food type and only pull out what you need for the day or meal for reheating and eating.

Option 2: Separate all of your prepped food into individual meals.

We recommend sticking to Option 1 for two reasons. First, you may not have the space in the refrigerator for that many containers. Second, you may not have enough containers to have all of your food separated by meal.

If you do opt for Option 2, this is where your mason jars can come in handy. At the beginning of the week you can prep your lunch for each day and have it ready to go!

Chapter 6

# Sample Builds

# Week 1 Example

| Day | SUN | MON | TUE | WED | THU | FRI | SAT |
|-----|-----|-----|-----|-----|-----|-----|-----|
| Breakfast | | Egg Cups | Egg Cups | Egg Cups | Egg Cups | Egg Cups | |
| Snack | | | | | | | |
| Lunch | | Shredded Beef, Squash & Broccoli | Shredded Beef, Squash & Broccoli | Shredded Beef, Squash & Broccoli | Shredded Beef, Squash & Broccoli | | |
| Snack | | | | | | | |
| Dinner | Shredded Beef | Chicken Stir Fry | Chicken Stir Fry | Salmon Filet and Asparagus | Salmon Filet and Asparagus | Turkey Burger with Avocado and Sweet Potato Fries | Restaurant |
| Snack | | | | | | | |

## Shopping List

| Produce | Dairy | Meats | Other | Supplements |
|---|---|---|---|---|
| Frozen Stir-Fry Veg. | Butter | Bacon | Pepperoncinis | Protein Powder |
| Garlic | Milk or Substitute | Eggs | Buns | Fish Oil |
| Rosemary | | Pot Roast | Sauce for Chicken | Probiotic |
| Thyme | | Boneless Chicken Breasts | Corn Starch | |
| Asparagus | | Pork Chops | EVOO | |
| Dill | | Salmon | Kosher Salt | |
| Lemon | | Italian Sausage | Oats | |
| Frozen Fruit | | Steak | Trail Mix | |
| Fresh Fruit | | | Nut Butter | |
| Salad Mix | | | | |
| Avocado | | | | |
| Broccoli | | | | |
| Squash | | | | |
| Potatoes | | | | |

# Week 2 Example

| Day | SUN | MON | TUE | WED | THU | FRI | SAT |
|---|---|---|---|---|---|---|---|
| Breakfast | | Egg Scramble | Egg Scramble | Egg Scramble | Egg Scramble | Egg Scramble | |
| Snack | | Trail Mix and Fruit | | | | | |
| Lunch | | Protein Salad and Fruit | Protein Salad and Fruit | Protein Salad and Fruit | Protein Salad and Fruit | | |
| Snack | | Protein Shake | | | | | |
| Dinner | Pulled Pork & Cole Slaw | Baked Pork Chop, Green Beans & Spinach | Baked Pork Chop, Green Beans & Spinach | Italian Sausage, Broccoli & Carrots | Italian Sausage, Broccoli & Carrots | Filet w/ Baked Brussels Sprouts & Sweet Potato Wedges | Restaurant |
| Snack | | | | | | | |

## *Shopping List*

| Produce | Dairy | Meats | Other |
|---|---|---|---|
| Frozen Veg Mix | Mayo | Eggs | ACV |
| Greens Mix | | Pork Shoulder | Ketchup |
| Fresh Fruit | | Italian Sausage | Brown Sugar |
| Green Beans | | Bacon | Chili Powder |
| Spinach | | | Paprika |
| Broccoli | | | Garlic Powder |
| Carrots | | | Onion Powder |
| Cole Slaw Mix | | | Cayenne Pepper |
| | | | Cumin |
| | | | Trail Mix |
| | | | |

# Week 3 Example

| Day | SUN | MON | TUE | WED | THU | FRI | SAT |
|---|---|---|---|---|---|---|---|
| Breakfast | | Egg Cups | Egg Cups | Egg Cups | Egg Cups | Egg Cups | |
| Snack | | | | | | | |
| Lunch | | Protein Salad and Fruit | Protein Salad and Fruit | Protein Salad and Fruit | Protein Salad and Fruit | | |
| Snack | | | | | | | |
| Dinner | Turkey Chili | Chicken Fajitas | Chicken Fajitas | Lamb chops | Lamb chops | Tilapia | Restaurant |
| Snack | | | | | | | |

## Shopping List

| Produce | Dairy | Meats | Other |
|---|---|---|---|
| Greens Mix | Pepper Jack Cheese | Eggs | Soy Sauce |
| Limes | Milk or Substitute | Turkey | White Beans |
| Cilantro | | Chicken | Chicken Stock |
| Bell Peppers | | Lamb | Trail Mix |
| Onion | | Tilapia | |
| Fresh Fruit | | Bacon | |
| Rosemary | | | |
| Thyme | | | |
| | | | |

# Week 4 Example

| Day | SUN | MON | TUE | WED | THU | FRI | SAT |
|---|---|---|---|---|---|---|---|
| Breakfast | | Egg Scramble | Egg Scramble | Egg Scramble | Egg Scramble | Egg Scramble | |
| Snack | | | | | | | |
| Lunch | | Protein Salad and Fruit | Protein Salad and Fruit | Protein Salad and Fruit | Protein Salad and Fruit | | |
| Snack | | | | | | | |
| Dinner | Beefy Pasta Sauce & Green Beans, Spinach, Squash | Beefy Pasta Sauce & Green Beans, Spinach, Squash | Beefy Pasta Sauce & Green Beans, Spinach, Squash | Chicken & Broccoli, carrots | Chicken & Broccoli, carrots | Dude Burgers & Roasted Sweet Potatoes | Restaurant |
| Snack | | | | | | | |

## *Shopping List*

| Produce | Dairy | Meats | Other |
|---|---|---|---|
| Frozen Veg. | Grated Parm | Eggs | Honey |
| Onion | Mozzarella cheese | Ground Beef | Ginger Powder |
| Garlic | | Chicken Breast | Sesame Oil |
| Fresh Fruit | | | Italian Seasoning |
| Broccoli | | | Hamburger Buns |
| Green Beans | | | Trail Mix |
| Spinach | | | |
| Carrots | | | |
| Orange juice | | | |
| Mushrooms | | | |
| | | | |
| | | | |

Part II

# Getting to Work

# Step-by-Step Recipes

# Snacks

## *Shakes*

Shakes are a great option if you have limited time and need calories and a complete macronutrient profile. They can be made in the morning and taken with you to work as long as they are refrigerated. They can also be consumed during your commute with little attention and no utensils or cleanup needed!

### Fruit

Frozen fruit

Banana

Berries

Peaches

Pineapple

### Greens

Spinach

Kale

Mixed greens

### Liquid

Milk or kefir

Water

Coconut milk

Almond/Cashew milk

### Protein

Whey

Egg

Plant-based

### Fats

Nut butter

Coconut oil

Avocado oil

Chia seeds

### Flavor

Cinnamon

Vanilla

Cacoa

Coconut

# Nuts

You can always select nuts from the list below and just snack on those. If you want to have more variety of flavor, texture, and nutrients, I recommend making your own trail mix and combining it with dried fruits of your choice.

## *Trail Mix*

Make your own trail mix! Pick three to five things that you like and combine. Our formula is something salty, something sweet and various dried fruits.

| **Nuts** | **Dried Fruit** |
|---|---|
| Almonds | Cherries |
| Walnuts | Raisins |
| Cashews | Blueberries |
| Peanuts | Banana chips |
| Pistachios | Apples |
| Pecans | Apricots |
| Pine | **Extras** |
| **Seeds** | Chocolate (dark, milk, or white) |
| Pumpkin | Pretzels |
| Sunflower | Peanut butter chips |
| Flax | Granola |
| Hemp | Popcorn |

### Dave's Mix

Cashews

Dried apples

Dried bananas

Dried apricots

Mix Ingredients in bowl and store in Ziploc bag or Tupperware®.

### Fruit

Most of the following fruits can be consumed whole or you can prep them and combine them to make a fruit salad. This can be a great pairing to go with your trail mix. Always make sure to thoroughly wash any fruit that will be consumed with the skin on.

| | |
|---|---|
| Apples | Oranges |
| Pears | Mandarin oranges |
| Grapes | Pineapple |
| Mixed berries | Watermelon |
| Kiwi | Sliced melon |
| Bananas | |

#### <u>Favorite Fruit Salad</u>

1 quart strawberries

1 pineapple or 2 20-ounce cans pineapple chunks

1 pint blueberries

Remove tops of strawberries with paring knife. Cut strawberries in half lengthwise (or smaller if desired). Cut top and bottom off of pineapple. Drain canned pineapple; if using a whole pineapple, cut into ½ -inch chunks, making sure to remove the firm core and rough skin. Mix ingredients in bowl and store in Ziploc bag or Tupperware®.

# Popcorn

Popcorn is a great snack if you want something light and crunchy. You can dress it up with all sorts of different flavor combinations from salty to sweet. To make your own popcorn at home, you can always use an air fryer if you have one, or you can improvise on your own.

## Ingredients

¼ cup popcorn kernels

1 teaspoon canola oil

1 brown paper bag

1 tablespoon butter

Salt to taste

## Directions

1. Heat butter in a small microwave safe dish for 30-45 seconds or until melted.
2. Stir and set to the side.
3. Add kernels and canola oil to paper bag.
4. Fold the top of the bag a couple times to close.
5. Place in the microwave folded side down.
6. Cook on high 2-3 minutes or until kernels stop popping.
7. Transfer to large bowl, slowly drizzle with butter and sprinkle with salt to taste.

# Breakfast

## *Eggs*

### <u>Scrambled</u>

Crack eggs into a bowl, add about 1 ounce of milk or heavy whipping cream to bowl for each egg. The dairy is optional but recommended for fluffier eggs. Add a little bit of salt and as much pepper as you like, mix with a whisk or a fork.

Heat 1-2 tablespoons of butter over medium-low heat and let foam. Add eggs to pan and move around with a spatula until finished. With scrambled eggs, it's important to remember this adage from Alton Brown, "Done in the pan means overdone on the plate."

### <u>Omelet</u>

Crack as many eggs as you want in a bowl and add some salt and pepper. Stir the eggs to break up the yolks. The amount of eggs you have will dictate the size of pan you need.

Heat 1-2 tablespoons of butter over medium-low heat and let foam. Pour eggs into the pan and rotate the pan around to keep eggs cooking evenly. Once most of the eggs are set, add any ingredients you like down the middle third—not too much, though, or the omelet will break. Use spatula to fold over ⅓ of the omelet over the ingredients, then repeat on other side. I also then like to flip the omelet over to ensure even cooking before serving.

## Additional Omelet and Scrambled ingredients

| Diced Veggies | Meat | Shredded Cheese |
|---|---|---|
| Onion | Ham | Monterey Jack |
| Garlic | Bacon | Swiss |
| Tomato | Sausage | Cheddar |
| Broccoli | | Provolone |
| Mushroom | | |
| Bell peppers | | |

# Fried Eggs

Melt 1-2 tablespoons butter over low heat and let foam. Add eggs to pan as you see fit.

**Over Easy**—Let whites set and then gently flip with a spatula. Yolk should be runny when served.

**Over Medium**—Let whites set and gently flip with a spatula. Yolks should be firm, but only slightly runny.

**Over Hard**—Let whites set and gently flip with a spatula. Yolks should be firm. If I am going to cook my eggs over hard, I will break the yolk right before I flip it.

**Basted**—Go with 2-3 tablespoons of butter in the pan. Crack eggs in pan and let white set. Gently tilt the pan and start spooning the hot butter over the eggs until cooked.

# Boiled Eggs

Put as many eggs as you need in one layer in a pot. Cover with water and add salt. Cover the pot and cook on high until the water boils. Remove from heat and let stand for 12 minutes. Dump into colander and run cold water over the eggs for 2-3 minutes. If you're not going to eat the eggs immediately, we recommended leaving the shells intact; peeled eggs tend to get rubbery if they sit too long.

I also recommend buying eggs and letting them sit in the refrigerator until the day of or before the sell-by date. This will make them easier to peel, as there is a membrane that helps keep the egg and yolk from moving around the shell. This membrane degrades over time.

# Baked Egg Cups

## Ingredients

12 slices bacon or 1 pound breakfast sausage

1 dozen eggs

## Prep

Separate 12 slices of bacon

## Directions for bacon

1. Preheat oven to 400°.
2. In muffin pan, wrap one slice of bacon around inside edge of each cup.
3. Bake in oven 15-18 minutes or until bacon is three-quarters cooked to your liking (longer for crispier bacon).
4. Remove muffin pan from oven.
5. Crack 1 egg into each cup.
6. Sprinkle with salt and pepper (optional).
7. Bake in the oven again for 10-15 minutes, depending on desired egg doneness (I like to wait until the tops are entirely white.

## Directions for sausage

1. Preheat oven to 400°.
2. Brown sausage in small skillet until evenly browned and drain.
3. Grease muffin pan well and sprinkle sausage evenly in each muffin well.
4. Crack one egg in each muffin well and sprinkle with salt and pepper (optional).
5. Bake in oven for 10-15 minutes, depending on egg doneness (I like to wait until the tops are entirely white).

# Cold Oats

## Ingredients

4 ounces almond milk

1.5 ounces old-fashioned oats

## Directions

1. Combine ingredients and let sit in the refrigerator overnight.

## Toppings

Choose what you like

### Maple brown sugar

- 1 tablespoon maple syrup

- ½ tablespoon brown sugar

- 1 teaspoon cinnamon

### Fruit

- Top with your choice of fresh or dried fruit

# Blueberry Banana Pancakes

## Ingredients

2 ripe bananas

2 eggs

1/2 cup instant oats

1 teaspoon vanilla extract

1 teaspoon cinnamon

1 cup fresh blueberries or frozen fruit

## Prep

Smash bananas in a bowl or use hand mixer until smooth.

Whisk eggs and vanilla in separate bowl.

Mix eggs, vanilla, oats, cinnamon, and bananas thoroughly.

## Directions

1. Warm a medium-sized pan with butter or oil of your choice.

2. Add approximately 1/2 cup of mixture to pan, making sure to flatten out the middle if necessary.

3. Allow to cook until the edges become firm and bubbles escape the mixture.

4. Carefully flip and cook another one to two minutes.

Garnish with fresh blueberries. If using frozen fruit, use microwave safe bowl and heat for 30 seconds, mix, and allow to sit while cooking pancakes. Use real maple syrup or honey and enjoy!

# Lunch

# Mason Jar Salads

Here is a great way to prep your salads for the week. Use the salad base below or vary it however you'd like. Combine with the protein and quality oil blend of your choice. Mix and match different flavors to find what works for you.

The steps are as follows:

1. Add chopped veggies to the bottom of the mason jar.
2. Add about 2 tablespoons of a healthy dressing.
3. Layer in one serving of your favorite protein.
4. Layer your greens mix on top.

Now your salads are ready to go for the week. Keep them in the fridge and take them as you need them. When you're ready to eat, just unscrew the top and carefully empty the jar onto a plate or bowl, and bam! You'll have your salad base, with protein on top, followed by veggies and dressing.

*Note—You can use any of the combinations below for mason jar salads; however, you would not need to reheat any of your protein selections separately.

# Salad Base

## Ingredients

12-ounce bag mixed greens, spinach, or baby spring greens—anything but iceberg

3 bell peppers (various) colors

1 medium onion

1 cucumber

1 8-ounce container mushrooms

1 pint of grape or cherry tomatoes

Something crunchy: sunflower kernels, pepitas, croutons, almonds, etc.

Feel free to add or subtract any ingredients based on your own preference.

## Prep

Wash greens and vegetables.

Chop or slice vegetables based on preference.

Store in separate containers.

## Directions

Place as much or as little of each ingredient you like into a bowl.

# Shredded Beef Salad

## Ingredients

3 ounces shredded beef (see shredded beef recipe)

Salad mix

## Directions

Reheat shredded beef until it is just warm.

Mix with your salad.

# Fajita Salad

## Ingredients

Leftover fajita meat and peppers

Salad Mix

## Directions

Reheat fajita mix until it is warm and mix with your salad.

# Tuna Salad

## Ingredients

1 can tuna

1-2 tablespoons mustard or mayo

1 rib of celery

½ small red onion

Juice of ½ lemon

Black pepper

Salt

## Prep

Open and drain 1 can of tuna.

Slice celery.

Measure 1-2 tablespoons of mayo or mustard (amount and choice is up to you).

Chop onion.

## Directions

1. In a bowl, mix ingredients.
2. Add salt and pepper to taste.
3. Serve over salad or on a sandwich.

# Spinach and Pulled Pork Salad

## Ingredients

3 ounces pulled pork (see recipe)

2 cups spinach

1 granny smith apple

¼ cup cherry tomatoes

¼ cucumber

¼ cup walnuts

## Prep

Chop apple

Slice cucumber

Wash spinach

Reheat pulled pork

## Directions

Add all ingredients to bowl and mix.

# Shrimp Salad

## Ingredients—Makes 3 servings

1 bag of 20-40 peeled, deveined, and cooked shrimp

Juice of 1 lemon

1 teaspoon garlic powder

1 teaspoon thyme

1 teaspoon kosher salt

3 tablespoons EVOO

## Prep

Defrost shrimp.

Measure out herbs and spices and EVOO and combine in bowl.

Juice lemon and add to shrimp mix.

## Directions

Combine ingredients in bowl and mix thoroughly.

## Dressing

6 ounces dressing base (see below)

2 cloves garlic

1 lemon

1 teaspoon thyme

1 teaspoon kosher salt

## Prep

Mince garlic.

## Directions

Combine ingredients in shaker and shake thoroughly until combined.

# Quality Oil Blends

## Dressing Base

## Ingredients

4 ounces EVOO

2 ounces vinegar (ACV, red wine vinegar or balsamic)

1 Tablespoon brown mustard

## Directions

Combine ingredients in shaker and shake thoroughly to combine.

# Dave's Dressing

## Ingredients

2 cloves garlic

½ teaspoon cumin

½ teaspoon chili powder

Juice of 1 lime

½ cup chopped cilantro

## Prep

Mince cilantro and garlic

Make Dressing Base

## Directions

Combine ingredients in shaker and shake thoroughly to combine.

# Greek Dressing

Good when using gyros for salad protein

## Ingredients

- 1 serving dressing base
- 2 cloves garlic
- 1 teaspoon marjoram
- 1 teaspoon rosemary
- 1 teaspoon kosher salt

## Prep

Make dressing base.

Mince garlic.

Measure ingredients.

## Directions

Combine ingredients in shaker and shake thoroughly to combine.

# Italian Dressing

## Ingredients

Dressing Base made with red wine vinegar

2 cloves garlic

1 teaspoon Italian seasoning

1 teaspoon oregano

1 teaspoon kosher salt

## Prep

Make dressing base.

Mince garlic.

Measure ingredients.

## Directions

Combine ingredients in shaker and shake thoroughly to combine.

# Dinner

# Proteins

# Beef

# Steak Marinade

## Ingredients

Juice of 1 lemon

⅓ cup soy sauce

½ cup olive oil

¼ cup Worcestshire sauce

3 cloves minced garlic

1 teaspoon pepper

3 tablespoons dried basil

2 tablespoons dried parsley

## Directions

1. Combine all ingredients in bowl and mix thoroughly.

2. Transfer to Ziploc bag and add steak.

3. Marinate in refrigerator for one to three hours.

# Beef and Vegetable Soup

## Ingredients

1 box beef stock

2 carrots

1 can of sweet corn

2 potatoes

1 pound stew beef

1 teaspoon thyme

1 teaspoon rosemary

1 teaspoon marjoram

## Prep

Peel and slice carrots.

Dice potatoes into ¼-inch cubes.

Measure out spices.

Open can of corn.

## Directions

1. Pour beef stock into pot, turn to medium heat.

2. Add potatoes and beef. Bring to a boil, reduce heat to low.

3. Add remaining ingredients.

4. Simmer 3-4 hours.

5. Add salt pepper or spices to taste.

# Bacon-Wrapped Filet Mignon

## Ingredients

2 Filet Mignon

2 strips of bacon

Kosher Salt

Pepper

## Prep

Salt and pepper both sides of filets.

Bring to room temperature for two hours, flipping after first hour.

## Directions

1. Preheat oven to 400° with cast iron skillet inside oven.

2. Once heated, place skillet on high heat add enough oil to coat bottom of pan.

3. Sear filets for 45 seconds each side.

4. Place back in oven for a minute and a half on 1:30 each side (if you like your beef more than medium rare, buy ribeye or T-bone instead).

5. Take skillet out of oven, move filets to cooling rack for 3 minutes and serve.

# Beef Pasta Sauce

## Ingredients

2 pounds ground beef

2 tablespoons olive oil

1 large onion

2 32-ounce cans whole peeled tomatoes

2 6-ounce cans tomato paste

2 cloves garlic

½ tablespoon Italian seasoning

½ tablespoon oregano

1 tablespoon coarse kosher salt

1 tablespoon chili powder

2 bay leaves

1 teaspoon red pepper flakes, optional

1 tablespoon sugar, optional

## Prep

Dice onion.

Chop garlic.

Combine spices in small bowl.

Open all cans.

## Directions

1. Heat 2 tablespoons olive oil in large 12" skillet.
2. Add diced onion and garlic, 2 teaspoons kosher salt, sauté onions until golden brown.
3. Add ground beef to onions and garlic and cook until and browned.
4. Add tomatoes and paste, reduce to simmer, add spices to taste.
5. Simmer on stove at least 4 hours, stirring periodically.

# The Dude Burger

## Ingredients

2 pounds ground beef

1 egg

3 cloves garlic minced

1/2 cup chopped onion

3/4 cup shredded parmesan cheese

1 teaspoon Italian seasoning

## Prep

1. Lightly beat egg.

2. Chop onion.

3. Mince garlic.

4. In a large mixing bowl, fold egg, garlic and onion into ground beef.

5. Combine Italian seasoning and parmesan in separate bowl.

6. Fold dry ingredients into ground beef.

7. Separate beef into portions about tennis ball size.

8. Flatten into 3/4 -inch patties while using your palm to create a defined edges.

## Directions

1. Cook on the grill or in a pan how you like them done (medium-rare, medium, well).

# Chicken

# Chicken and Broccoli

## Ingredients

## Marinade:

½ cup soy sauce or Bragg's Liquid Aminos

¼ cup honey

2 cloves garlic

1 tablespoon ginger powder

½ tablespoon cumin

½ teaspoon red pepper flake, optional

1 tablespoon sesame oil, optional

¼ cup of some sort of acid, optional (OJ or rice wine vinegar)

2 pieces boneless skinless chicken (breast or thigh)

1 medium head of broccoli or one bag of frozen broccoli

## Prep

Combine soy sauce with honey in bowl; stir in acid (OJ, rice wine vinegar).

Add Ginger, garlic, Cumin, Red Pepper Flake (optional) to liquid mix and stir.

Cut chicken into cubes or slices, whatever you prefer.

Place in marinade for 30-45 minutes prior to cooking.

Chop (if necessary) or cook broccoli.

## Directions

1. Preheat 10" skillet on med-high heat with enough oil to coat bottom of pan.
2. Add chicken to pan, stirring occasionally until cooked.
3. Add cooked broccoli to pan.
4. Add 1 tablespoon of sesame oil and toss to coat (optional).

# Fajitas

## Ingredients

3-4 boneless skinless chicken breasts or 1 pound skirt steak

½ cup olive oil

⅓ cup soy sauce

½ teaspoon cumin

½ teaspoon chili powder

½ teaspoon red pepper flakes

2 cloves garlic

Juice of 1 lime

½ bunch cilantro, chopped

2 tablespoons brown sugar

3 bell peppers

1 large onion

Pinch of salt

## Prep

In bowl or gallon Ziploc, combine olive oil, soy sauce, lime juice and spices.

Place chicken breasts or skirt steak in marinade for 1 hour.

Slice bell peppers and onions.

## Directions

1. Preheat grill or grill pan to med-high heat. Place cast iron skillet on grill or top of stove on med-high heat.

2. Grill chicken or skirt steak on either grill or grill pan.

3. While chicken is grilling, place oil in cast iron, salt, and caramelize peppers and onions.

4. Remove chicken from grill, let stand five minutes.

5. Slice chicken or skirt steak against the grain and serve.

# Chicken Tacos

## Ingredients

1 pound ground meat (beef, chicken or turkey)

2 tablespoons chili powder

1 tablespoon cumin

2 teaspoons cornstarch

2 teaspoons kosher salt

2 teaspoons garlic powder

1½ teaspoons paprika

½ teaspoon cayenne (optional)

Water

Hard or soft taco shells

Garnishes: shredded lettuce, diced tomatoes, shredded cheddar cheese, sour cream

## Prep

Combine spices in jar or bowl and mix well.

Have large glass of water ready.

## Directions

1. Preheat 12" skillet over medium heat with enough oil to coat bottom of pan.
2. Brown ground meat.
3. Drain excess fat from pan.
4. Place pan back over medium heat.
5. Add about ⅔ of spice mixture.
6. Stir to combine, adding water as necessary.
7. Add remaining spice mixture and more water if necessary.
8. Stir until thoroughly mixed and serve.

# Chicken Stir Fry

## Ingredients

2 boneless skinless chicken breasts or thighs

1 bag frozen stir fry veggies

1 bottle of stir fry sour sauce, orange, sweet and sour, General Tso's, whatever you like

1/2 cup corn starch

## Prep

Cut chicken into strips or cubes.

Lightly coat chicken pieces evenly with corn starch.

Open sauce and set to the side.

## Directions

1. Preheat 12" skillet on high with enough oil to coat pan.
2. Cook chicken in skillet, moving around to ensure even cooking and browning.
3. Cook frozen veggies in microwave.
4. Open and drain excess water from veggies.
5. Toss veggies in pan once chicken is done cooking.
6. Add about ½ jar of your sauce of choice.
7. Toss to coat and serve.

# Basic Chicken Wings

## Ingredients

Package whole chicken wings (about 8-10 wings)

## Prep

Split drum from wing piece (optional).

Spread wings and drums over steamer basket (you may need to steam in multiple batches).

Place large pot with 1" of liquid (water OR see sauce recipes, below) over high heat and bring to a boil.

## Directions

1. Place steamer basket with wings in pot and cover. cook for 10 minutes. Note: if doing multiple batches, you may need to add liquid to pot between batches.

2. Let wings cool on counter for 20 minutes.

3. Preheat oven to 425°.

4. Thoroughly spray baking sheet with non-stick spray and add wings.

5. Cook wings for 20 minutes; 6. flip wings and cook for 20 more minutes.

7. Add wings to your sauce of choice in large mixing bowl and toss to coat thoroughly

# "Buffalo Style" Sauce

## Ingredients

6 tablespoons unsalted butter

½ cup hot sauce

Pinch of kosher salt

## Prep

Melt butter.

Measure salt and hot sauce.

## Directions

1. Combine ingredients and mix.

2. Bonus: I like to steam my "Buffalo Style" wings with an IPA-style beer instead of water.

# BBQ Wings

## Ingredients

6 tablespoons unsalted butter

½ cup BBQ sauce

Pinch of kosher salt

## Prep

Melt butter.

Measure salt and BBQ sauce.

## Directions

1. Combine ingredients and mix.

2. Bonus: I like to steam my BBQ wings with a brown ale-Style beer instead of water.

# Hot BBQ Wings

## Ingredients

6 tablespoons unsalted butter

¼ cup BBQ sauce

¼ cup hot sauce

Pinch of kosher salt

## Prep

Melt butter.

Measure salt, hot sauce and BBQ sauce.

## Directions

1. Combine ingredients and mix.
2. Bonus: I like to steam my Hot BBQ style wings with a light beer instead of water.

# Fish

# Clam Chowder

## Ingredients

3 cups heavy whipping cream

3 potatoes

1 can of clams

4 slices bacon

1 medium onion

## Prep

Dice potatoes into ¼" cubes.

Cut bacon into ¼" pieces.

Dice onion.

Measure out cream.

Open can of clams.

## Directions

1. Cook bacon in large pot over medium heat.

2. Remove cooked bacon, set aside.

3. Sweat onions in bacon grease.

4. Add potatoes and cream.

5. Bring to a boil.

6. Turn heat to low, simmer 10-15 minutes until potatoes are soft.

7. Add canned clams and cook for 20 minutes.

8. Serve in bowls and garnish with bacon bits.

# Salmon Fillet

## Ingredients

Salmon fillet

Kosher salt

3-4 tablespoons Butter

Dried dill (preferably with a "shaker" top)

1 lemon

## Prep

Bring salmon to room temperature.

Slice butter into about 10-14 thin slices (for whole fillet).

Slice 5 thin slices of lemon.

## Directions

### Individual Piece—Pan Seared

1. Season both sides of salmon with salt and dill (only flesh side if you still have the skin on).
2. Place 10" skillet on stove.
3. Place 1 tablespoon butter in skillet. Turn heat to medium.
4. Let butter foam.
5. Place salmon in hot skillet (flesh side down if you still have the skin on).
6. Let cook for 2-3 minutes depending on thickness of piece (closer to the tail tends to be thinner).
7. Flip and cook for 2-3 minutes depending on thickness of piece.
8. Plate and squeeze lemon juice on fish.

## Whole Side—Oven Baked

1. Thinly slice lemon (5 total slices).
2. Preheat oven to 475°.
3. Cut a piece of foil big enough to wrap fillet in.
4. Slice 10-14 thin pieces of butter.
5. Arrange half of the pieces of butter on foil so that the salmon will lay on top of all slices.
6. Place fillet skin side down on butter slices.
7. Season with dill.
8. Use remaining butter slices to cover top of salmon evenly.
9. Place lemon slices on top of butter on salmon evenly.
10. Fold foil around salmon like a pouch.
11. Bake in oven for 30-40 minutes.

# Parmesan Crusted Tilapia

## Ingredients

2-3 pieces of tilapia

1 egg

1 tablespoon water

1/4 cup grated parmesan

## Prep

Pat tilapia dry with paper towel.

Crack egg into a flat-bottomed container; add water.

Stir egg and water until combined.

Place parmesan in a second flat-bottomed container.

Preheat oven to 375°.

Spray baking sheet with cooking spray.

## Directions

1. Dip tilapia into egg mix, coat both sides, shake off excess.

2. Coat tilapia in parmesan cheese.

3. Place on baking sheet.

4. Cook in oven for 10 minutes per side.

# Turkey

# Turkey Burger

## Ingredients

1 pound ground turkey

1 egg

2 tablespoons parmesan cheese

1 tablespoon parsley

½ tablespoon oregano

½ tablespoon thyme

1 tablespoon avocado oil

## Prep

Measure spices and cheese and combine in a small bowl.

Place ground turkey in large mixing bowl.

## Directions

1. Combine spices and cheese with ground turkey in mixing bowl.
2. Mix gently with hands.
3. Form patties.
4. Grill dem bad boys (add cheese, feta or goat cheese if you're feeling fancy).

# Turkey Meatballs

## Ingredients

1 pound ground meat

1 tablespoon Italian seasoning

½ tablespoon kosher salt

2 tablespoons grated parmesan cheese

1 egg

## Prep

Place meat in bowl.

Add spices, cheese, and egg to meat.

Mix and then roll into balls about the size of a golf ball.

## Directions

1. Preheat pan over medium-high heat, with enough oil to coat bottom of pan.

2. Add meatballs around the outside of the pan, leaving space in between.

3. Get a good sear, about 30-45 seconds.

4. Roll meatballs to different side.

5. Repeat steps 3 and 4 until meatballs have been seared on all sides.

6. Serve with red sauce and pasta or let cool and freeze for later use.

# Pork & Lamb

# Pork or Lamb Chops

## Ingredients

4-6 lamb chops or 1-2 medium-size pork chops

¼ cup olive oil

1 clove garlic

2 pinches kosher salt

Rosemary

Thyme

## Prep

Salt and bring lamb chops to room temperature.

Mince garlic.

Combine EVOO, garlic, rosemary, and thyme in bowl.

## Directions

1. Preheat Oven to 405° with cast iron skillet inside.

2. Brush olive oil mix onto both sides of lamb chops.

3. Once oven is heated, remove cast iron (use an oven mitt!) and place on stovetop burner on high.

4. Place lamb chops in pan, leaving plenty of space in between.

5. Sear for 45 seconds and flip, sear for 45 more seconds.

6. Place skillet and lamb chops back in oven for 1 minute, then flip for 1 minute.

7. Pull skillet from oven and place lamb chops on cooling rack for 3 minutes.

# Gyros

## Ingredients

1 pound ground lamb

2 cloves garlic

½ tablespoon marjoram

½ tablespoon rosemary

1 teaspoon kosher salt

Pita bread

Optional garnishes: chopped onion, chopped tomato, feta cheese

## Prep

Mince garlic.

Measure out spices and salt.

Add spices and garlic to food processor.

Add meat to food processor.

Process until fine paste (1-2 minutes).

You can skip the food processor, but your final product will be more like meatloaf.

Form meat into a loaf (if you have a loaf pan, grease it and press meat into it).

## Directions

1. Preheat oven 325°.

2. Bake loaf in oven for 40-50 minutes.

3. Slice and serve on pita bread with gyro sauce (recipe follows) and garnishes of choice

# Gyro Sauce

## Ingredients

1 medium cucumber

2 cups Greek yogurt plain

4 cloves garlic

1 tablespoon olive oil

2 teaspoon vinegar (red wine preferred, ACV acceptable)

## Prep

Peel cucumber, slice in half the long way.

Use spoon to scoop out the seeds and dice cucumber.

Measure out ingredients.

## Directions

1. Put ingredients in bowl and stir to combine.

2. Let stand covered in refrigerator for 2-3 hours (overnight is best).

3. Adjust flavors as needed.

# Super BLT Sandwich

## Ingredients

2 slices cooked bacon

1 healthy serving of sliced turkey

1-2 leaves of romaine lettuce

2 tomato slices

4-5 thin cucumber slices

½ avocado, sliced or smashed

Mayo or mustard

Sprouts

# Beer Brats

## Ingredients

Brats

1 onion

1 green pepper

2 cans of light beer

## Prep

Slice onion and pepper.

Place beer in a 2 quart pot.

Add peppers and onions to beer.

## Directions

1. Simmer beer, onion, and peppers on low.

2. Grill brats.

3. Place brats in beer and simmer 5-10 Minutes.

# Slow Cooker Recipes

# Pulled Pork

## Ingredients

1½ -2 pound pork butt or shoulder

½ cup apple cider vinegar

½ cup ketchup

⅓ cup brown sugar

1 tablespoon kosher salt

2 tablespoons chili powder

1 teaspoon paprika

1 teaspoon garlic powder

1 teaspoon onion powder

½ teaspoon cayenne pepper (optional)

½ teaspoon cumin

## Prep

Open pork package and place in slow cooker, fat side up.

Measure ACV, ketchup and brown sugar and mix in small bowl.

Measure remaining ingredients and add to ketchup mixture.

## Directions

1. Cover pork butt in spice mixture.
2. Cook on low 8 hours.
3. Remove pork from slow cooker, place on cutting board.
4. Shred with two forks.
5. Place shredded pork back into juices in slow cooker and stir.

# Turkey Chili

## Ingredients

1 pound ground turkey

3 cans white beans

32 ounces of chicken stock

8 ounces pepper jack cheese

1 large onion

2 cloves garlic

2 teaspoons cumin

Kosher salt

Pepper

## Prep

Open cans and chicken stock.

Chop onion.

Mince garlic.

Grate cheese if bought in block.

Measure out spices.

## Directions

1. Preheat 12" skillet on medium heat, add enough oil to coat bottom.
2. Sweat onions (cook until translucent), add a pinch of salt.
3. Move onions to slow cooker.
4. Put skillet back over the heat and brown turkey with pinch of salt.
5. Drain turkey, then add to slow cooker.
6. Add beans and stock to slow cooker, stir to combine.

7. Add garlic and cumin and stir.

8. Cook on low 4-6 hours.

9. Add cheese, stir until melted.

10. Add salt and pepper to taste and serve.

# Shredded Beef

## Ingredients

1-2 pound chuck or pot roast

1 jar of sliced pepperoncinis

## Prep

Place chuck roast in slow cooker.

Pour pepperoncinis over the top of the roast.

## Directions

1. Cook on low 8 hours.

2. Remove chuck from slow cooker, shred with forks.

3. Place shredded meat back in slow cooker, turn to warm.

# Vegetables

# Baked Cauliflower

## Ingredients

½ cup Greek yogurt

1 tablespoon chili powder

½ tablespoon garlic powder

½ tablespoon onion powder

1 teaspoon cumin

2 tablespoons olive oil

1 head cauliflower

## Prep

Preheat oven to 450°.

Slice stem off bottom of cauliflower head so that it can sit flat on a baking sheet.

Mix yogurt, spices, and olive oil in a bowl.

Spread yogurt mix onto cauliflower head.

## Directions

Place cauliflower in oven and bake 45 minutes.

# Green Beans

## Ingredients

1 bunch fresh green beans

Kosher salt

2 slices of bacon

Herbs and spices of your choice

## Prep

Trim stems of green beans.

Cut bacon into ¼" pieces.

## Directions

1. Preheat 12" skillet.

2. Cook bacon until it is about three-quarters cooked.

3. Add green beans to skillet.

4. Toss green beans, spreading bacon grease as evenly as possible.

5. Cook for 8-10 minutes, moving green beans around pan occasionally.

# Roasted Asparagus

## Ingredients

1 bunch asparagus

Kosher salt

EVOO

Herbs and spices of your choice

## Prep

Preheat oven to 400°

Trim bottom fifth of asparagus (the "woody" part; it will easily snap off, too)

Clean and rinse asparagus

## Directions

1. Spread asparagus over baking sheet.

2. Sprinkle with EVOO, salt and spices.

3. Place in oven for 8-10 minutes.

4. Move asparagus around baking sheet with tongs.

5. Cook for another 8-10 minutes.

# Roasted Brussels Sprouts

## Ingredients

1 bag or stalk of brussels sprouts (remove from stalk if necessary)

Kosher salt

EVOO

Herbs and spices of your choice

## Prep

Preheat oven to 400°.

Rinse brussels sprouts.

Trim bottom, halve vertically and remove any bad leaves.

## Directions

1. Spread brussels sprouts over baking sheet.

2. Sprinkle with EVOO, salt and spices.

3. Place in oven for 8-10 minutes.

4. Move brussels sprouts around sheet with tongs.

5. Cook for another 8-10 minutes.

# Sautéed Spinach

## Ingredients

1 pound uncooked spinach

Kosher salt

4 slices of bacon

2 clove garlic

Herbs and spices of your choice

## Prep

Measure and wash spinach.

Slice bacon into ¼" pieces.

Mince garlic cloves.

## Directions

1. Preheat 12" skillet.

2. Cook bacon until it is about three-quarters cooked.

3. Add spinach to skillet.

4. Toss spinach, spreading bacon grease as evenly as possible.

5. Cook for 8-10 minutes, moving spinach around pan occasionally.

# Smashed Fingerling Potatoes

### Ingredients

½ bag fingerling potatoes

Olive oil

Salt

Rosemary

Thyme

### Prep

Wash potatoes.

### Directions

1. Heat 12" sauté pan over medium high heat with enough olive oil to coat.

2. Add fingerling potatoes to hot pan.

3. Move pan around to coat potatoes in oil.

4. Add seasonings to potatoes, shake to coat.

5. Cook 10-15 minutes, moving potatoes around pan to ensure even browning.

6. Use the bottom of a coffee cup to flatten each potato.

7. Bake an additional 5 minutes to brown slightly and serve.

# Vinegar Slaw

## Ingredients

Head of cabbage or bagged slaw mix

3 tablespoons apple cider vinegar

1 tablespoon brown sugar

3 Slices of bacon

Salt

Pepper

## Prep

Shred cabbage using a grater or slice.

Cook bacon until crispy.

Chop or crumble bacon.

Heat ACV over low heat and add brown sugar.

Stir until brown sugar is combined.

## Directions

1. Combine ingredients in bowl and mix.

2. Add salt and pepper to taste.

# Grains & Potatoes

# Baked Rice

## Ingredients

1 cup rice

2 cups water

Kosher salt

EVOO

## Prep

Measure out rice and place in baking pan.

Measure out water, place in small pot.

## Directions

1. Preheat oven to 400°.
2. Boil water, salt, EVOO.
3. Add rice to baking pan.
4. Add boiling water to baking pan.
5. Cover with foil.
6. Bake for 45 minutes.

Flavor options—Cilantro Lime.

# Fried Rice

## Ingredients

2 cups rice, cooked

1 egg

1 scallion, chopped

1/2 cup edamame (thaw if frozen)

2 tablespoons sesame oil

## Prep

Cook rice (see baked rice recipe).

Chop scallion.

Thaw and peel (if in shell) edamame.

Measure sesame oil

## Directions

1. Preheat skillet over high heat (get that shit rocket hot).
2. Add sesame oil.
3. Add rice and toss until golden brown.
4. Add scallions, egg and edamame.
5. Cook 2 minutes.
6. Serve.

# Pasta with Creamy Mushroom & Bacon Sauce

## Ingredients

Pasta (your choice)

1 - 8 ounce package button mushrooms (pre-sliced is okay)

2 cloves garlic

½ cup heavy cream

½ cup chicken broth

2 tablespoons red wine vinegar

2 slices bacon

## Prep

Cut bacon into ¼ inch strips.

Slice mushrooms.

Mince garlic.

## Directions

1. Cook pasta.
2. While the pasta is cooking, heat saucepan over medium heat.
3. Add bacon to pan and cook until about halfway done.
4. Add mushrooms and brown.
5. Add heavy cream, chicken broth, and vinegar to pan, bring to a boil.
6. Reduce heat to low and simmer until sauce thickens.
7. Drain the pasta.
8. Add cooked pasta to pan and combine.
9. Serve.

# Baked Potatoes

## Ingredients

Sweet or russet potatoes

Olive oil

Kosher salt

## Prep

Preheat oven to 350°.

Poke potatoes with fork 4-5 times on each side.

Rub with olive oil and lightly salt.

## Directions

1. Place on baking tray and cook for 60 minutes.

# Potato Wedges

## Ingredients

Russet or sweet potato

Olive oil

Salt

Herbs and spices

## Prep

Preheat oven to 425°.

Cut potatoes into eight long wedges (like steak fries).

Evenly coat potatoes in olive oil (we like to do this by drizzling some EVOO over a baking sheet and laying the potatoes down on their sides, shaking to coat and then flipping them).

Season wedges on both sides.

## Directions

1. Bake for 20 minutes.
2. Flip and bake 20 minutes more or until golden brown.

For Spicy Potato Wedges, sprinkle with salt, chili powder, garlic powder and red pepper flakes to taste.

For Herbed Potato Wedges, sprinkle with salt, oregano, rosemary and garlic powder to taste.

# Roasted Sweet Potatoes

## Ingredients

2 large sweet potatoes or yams

4 tablespoons olive or avocado oil

4 tablespoons brown sugar

Salt to taste

## Prep

Preheat oven to 425°.

Wash potatoes, cut off ends, and cut lengthwise into halves.

Chop into approximately ¾" pieces.

## Directions

1. Place potato pieces in large mixing bowl.
2. Add oil and mix with large spoon until evenly coated.
3. Add half of the brown sugar and mix, add remainder and mix again.
4. Spread pieces onto a large baking tray lined with foil.
5. Bake at 425° for 20 minutes.
6. Remove tray, flip pieces with tongs or spatula.
7. Bake an additional 20 minutes.

# Sweet Corn

## Ingredients

1-4 fresh ears of corn in husk

1-2 Tbsp butter per ear

Salt

## Prep

Peel corn and remove silk

Put a large pot of water on to boil

## Directions

1. Add peeled corn to boiling water.

2. Turn off burner and heat corn in water about 25 minutes or until soft.

3. Remove corn with tongs and spread butter all over it.

4. Lightly salt to taste.

# Dessert

# Apples and Peanut Butter

**Ingredients**

Granny smith apple

Peanut or almond butter

**Directions**

1. Slice or wedge apple.

2. Spread peanut or almond butter on top of each slice or use as dip.

# Yogurt and fruit

## Ingredients

½ cup plain or vanilla Greek yogurt

½ cup fresh or frozen fruit

## Directions

Add sliced or chopped fresh fruit to bowl. If fruit is frozen, heat in microwave-safe bowl for 30 seconds, add yogurt on top and mix.

# Ready for More?

We hope you have enjoyed reading **The Dude's Meal Prep Manual** and have broadened your understanding of eating for health and the process of food preparation. Let this serve as an instruction manual that you can refer to year-round for convenient and easy meals that taste great and are easy to make. Share what you have learned with your friends and family. Invite them over for meals and display your new cooking skills. Show them the book. Share the recipes and give copies as gifts to people you think could use some help in the cooking department or already love to cook and will put it to good use.

And don't forget . . . ladies love dudes who cook!

For questions or comments, you can reach us at the addresses listed below.

**Facebook:**

@iwilltrain

@DavidSnedden

**Instagram:**

@iwilltrain

@phenomsonly

**Email:**

Cooking@iwilltrain.com

d.snedden19@gmail.com

# About the Authors

## Brian Baker, C.S.C.S.

Brian has been a Personal Trainer and Strength Coach for over a decade. He specializes in functional training and corrective exercise. He has worked with people from all walks of life including leaders in business, entertainment, and tech. He is also the founder of I Will Train, a personal development organization specializing in exercise, nutrition, and mindset.

## David Snedden, R.S.C.C.

David is a professional Strength and Conditioning Coach. He holds a Master's Degree in Exercise Science and Human Nutrition. He has been working with athletes since 2005 and has worked in collegiate sports and Minor League Baseball.

Made in the USA
Columbia, SC
14 December 2019